Silent Treatment

How to Recognize Emotional Abuse, Heal, and Reclaim Your Voice

Sophia Bengal

Title: Silent Treatment: How to Recognize Emotional Abuse, Heal, and Reclaim Your Voice

Cover image: Monica Schröder

"Managing silence is more difficult than managing words."
-Georges Clemenceau–

For *Coco*

Contents

Introduction

"Your heart is like a block of ice..."

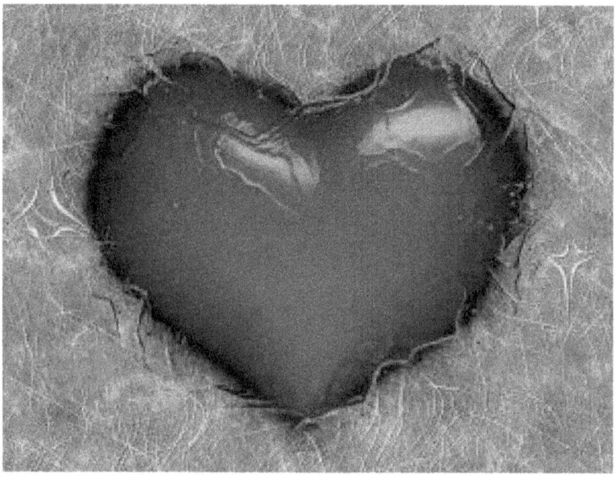

Have you ever argued with a partner or family member and, instead of solving the problem, ended up in a deadlock where one person completely shut down? Has your partner ever acted as if you didn't exist after a disagreement?

I'm sure that at some point We've all probably done something similar at some point — whether with a parent, sibling, partner, or even a friend. In anger, we choose to stop talking to them, pretending they aren't there and making them feel invisible. At first glance, it's "just" silence — but repeated over time, it can become a dangerous form of emotional and psychological abuse.

This is known as giving someone the silent treatment — a behavior in which a person deliberately ignores someone or refuses to respond to their questions or needs. It is so called because it's often used by people who seem emotionally cold and in control, but who are usually hiding deeper psychological, emotional, or communication problems.

However, it's important to distinguish between briefly refusing to speak after a quarrel and using the silent treatment as a repeated tactic to manipulate or control the other person. In this book, we'll explore situations where the silent treatment crosses into emotional and psychological abuse — and how to recognise and address it.

Silent treatment is a way of exerting power over someone — to control them, hurt them, and make our anger felt. It should not be confused with the decision to pause communication in order to calm a tense situation and return to the conversation when both sides are ready. Because silence can also be used manipulatively, we need to be aware of its effects and, when used intentionally, ensure it's for constructive purposes — to encourage calmer, healthier dialogue later.

Let's look at a few examples to see the difference more clearly:

Jessica never really knew what she had done to make her husband Alfred angry enough to stop speaking to her. She first experienced his silence when they were dating — after he saw her happily dancing with a friend. He left the club without a word and ignored her completely for weeks.

Over the years, Jessica grew used to her husband's cruel silences, still cooking, washing, and folding his clothes even while he ignored her for days or weeks. The silent treatment usually ended with Alfred initiating sex at night. The next morning, he behaved as though nothing had happened and refused to discuss it. Jessica could tell when he was angry: his expression hardened, signalling she should be extra submissive and avoid contradicting him. His voice became cold and distant, his smile disappearing.

She knew Alfred was deliberately trying to make her feel bad. Those silences and curt remarks made her anxious, and she worked even harder to please him — suppressing her own needs and desires.

Martin, 16, wanted a mobile phone for a school trip to Croatia. His father promised to pay half if Martin read a book he had given him, with Martin covering the rest from his savings. A few days before the phone was due to arrive, his father reminded him to finish the book. But Martin, just back from being out with friends, exploded — accusing his father of blackmail and of forcing him to do something he didn't want to do.

He shouted that not only would he refuse to read the book, but he also wouldn't do any of the other things his father had asked of him. His father said he would cancel the order, which enraged Martin even more. Refusing to rise to the provocation, his father closed his bedroom door and didn't speak to him until the next day. Martin stayed outside the door, shouting accusations of being ignored and manipulated, until exhaustion finally sent him to bed.

Being ignored is hard enough, but it's even worse when someone is angry and out of control (as in Martin's case), or when they are isolated through abuse and coercive control (as in Jessica's). These examples show that silence can be used with very different intentions: in one case, as a tool of emotional abuse; in the other, as a way to de-escalate a heated situation.

In conflict, as with a bruise, applying "ice" — calming the mind and cooling the situation — can help reduce the swelling of anger and pain. This helps us avoid blurting out things we don't truly mean — words spoken only to defend ourselves or to hurt the other person. This kind of temporary emotional distance, if used sparingly, can act as a painkiller — allowing both people to return to the conversation calmer and clearer-headed, rather than speaking in the heat of anger.

Human beings are very attached to our egos, and when someone criticizes us or questions our actions, our most frequent impulse is to react by attacking, even when we know they may be partly right. "Cooling off" means not talking about the issue for a while, distracting yourself, breathing, going for a walk (letting your partner know that you are leaving with the intention of talking again when you are calmer), writing in your journal, or talking to a friend who can help you verbalize the conflict and see it more clearly.

Be careful! We must bear in mind that keeping quiet is sometimes healthy, but only when there is a lot of excitement on one or both sides

CHAPTER 1

What is the silent treatment?

As we have already pointed out, it is important to distinguish between silence that is necessary to calm down and silence as abuse. Silence can occur between two people at a time when it is necessary to take time to analyze a problem and solve it, or in the case of an argument, to "calm the waters" before resuming dialogue and resolving the conflict. When the intention is to destabilize the other person, make them feel bad, blame them for something that is not their fault, or make them feel inferior, we are referring to the silent treatment as a form of **manipulation and abuse.**

The silent treatment is a type of **invisible violence** that is often used by narcissistic and/or toxic people to provoke a negative reaction in their victim. If used continuously, this silent treatment leaves victims with serious psychological scars. When it comes to the use of the silent treatment in the family environment, the consequences for the child or children who suffer this type of emotional abuse are quite painful and can lead to psychological problems in adulthood.

The Pain of Silence: The Neurobiological Evidence

The claim that silence can be painful is not merely a metaphor; it is a neurobiological reality. Scientific research has concluded that being ignored, excluded, or socially rejected activates the same brain regions that process physical pain. Specifically, the dorsal anterior cingulate cortex and the anterior insula, areas associated with the experience of pain, light up on brain scans when a person is ostracized. In simple terms, to the brain, social pain is real pain.

This reaction has deep evolutionary roots. For early humans, belonging to a group was essential for survival. Being expelled or rejected by the tribe was, in effect, a death sentence. Our modern brain, although living in a very different environment, retains this ancient wiring. When we perceive that an important social bond is in danger, the sympathetic nervous system is activated, triggering a stress response as if we were facing a physical threat.

This mechanism explains the intensity of the emotions experienced by the victim. Anxiety, distress, and despair are not an overreaction, but a response programmed by evolution to what the brain interprets as a serious threat to well-being. The silent treatment, therefore, is not a simple disagreement or miscommunication; it is a tactic that hijacks the victim's most basic survival instincts, turning silence into a form of psychological torture.

The silent treatment as emotional abuse

In clinical psychology, "the silent treatment" is considered another form of **psychological abuse or mistreatment through silence**. Accustomed as we are to more obvious and violent forms of abuse and mistreatment, it is often more difficult to identify as it is established as purely emotional abuse. The list of behaviors that we could consider emotional or psychological abuse is, unfortunately, quite long. Silence in emotional communication with our partner can be used as a terrible weapon of **psychological abuse.** This often occurs when one person has all the power over the other in a relationship and is aware of their emotional commitment. This is why we do not usually perceive this type of attitude as abuse. However, it is important and necessary to raise awareness of these types of attitudes, what they imply, and the damage they can cause.

Likewise, in addition to silence, there may be situations where such behavior is denied in a contradictory manner by saying that nothing is wrong while not even looking you in the face. Also, with phrases such as: "What do you mean? You're imagining things!" Or, in another phrase often used to convince victims that they are the problem, "you're being hysterical over nothing." This is when, although it appears to be a "milder" form of the silent treatment, it is actually turning into *gaslighting*. Gaslighting **is** another form of psychological abuse in which one attempts to manipulate the other person's perception of reality by denying reality, claiming that **something that** never happened did happen, or vice versa, and presenting false information in order to **make** the victim doubt their memory or perception.

People who use the silent treatment in their relationships show **immaturity and a lack of emotional intelligence**. They demonstrate **poor communication and conflict-resolution skills** when defending themselves. When you cannot or do not want to talk about what happened, the cause of the conflict can remain latent and unresolved. Furthermore, ignoring someone is to nullify and devalue them as a person. When the silence is so harsh and persistent that the victim does not know how to interpret what has happened or is really happening between them, and the other person persists even though they know this, we are dealing with a clear case of psychological abuse. In fact, the unconscious reasons why someone uses this tactic, such as punishment, anger, or disagreement, are one thing, but what the other person interprets from that behavior is quite another.

– It is impossible for you to communicate with him/her; he/she always puts up obstacles.

– After making a "mistake" and apologizing, nothing seems to be enough to make up for it, but they remain in the relationship with you.

– You feel distress and anxiety when you think that your bond/relationship could break at any moment and the other person could "abandon" you.

– You feel very sad, insignificant, and have very low self-esteem.

– You don't understand why they behave so harshly and blame you for everything. Often, you don't even know what caused their silence.

– In fact, you already feel guilty and responsible for the situation because you are trying to fix it without success.

– This is causing you to resort to medication or other substances such as anti-anxiety drugs, alcohol, or drugs.

– There is not only silence in verbal communication, but also emotional and physical isolation, denying you a hug or a kiss when they arrive or leave.

If you think several of these things are happening to you, be very careful because you could be suffering from the silent treatment.

How is the Silent Treatment applied?

Even if there is communication, sometimes the information the other person receives is doled out very sparingly. Other times, it is so convoluted or vague that it forces them to constantly doubt the emotional truth of what is being said. Silence in situations where an emotional response of some kind is demanded for a considerable amount of time is therefore a mechanism disguised as psychological abuse. When we refuse to listen to the other person, we are radically cutting off the possibility of clarifying misunderstandings, points of view, opinions, anger, or complaints.

A typical example of this situation is when communication is not in person and virtual communication is used, which is so common nowadays. In this context, it is much easier to avoid telling the whole truth or hiding our real feelings. This is when **resources** such as the following are often used:

– responding with **emoticons** instead of clear words or phrases, leading to doubts and misinterpretations on the part of the recipient.

– make an **excuse** so you don't have to respond right away

– **postpone the response** until later or to do it in person. This may never happen, or only if they feel truly compelled to do so by the other person's insistence.

Frequent use of these tactics is clear evidence that we are dealing with people who have **serious emotional deficits**, such as a **lack of empathy**. As verified by clinical psychology, this type of behavior not only denotes immaturity, pettiness, and a lack of emotional intelligence, but can also have serious effects on the other person.

Ignoring someone or giving them the silent treatment for hours or days can feel like **psychological torture**. The other person does not really know what is going through the mind of the "insensitive" person. It is very easy to fall into a cycle of guilt, trying to find an explanation for the silence. By remaining in doubt about what is going on in the other person's heart, the victim basically suffers from a simple lack of communication. They will keep thinking about the situation and looking for possible actions on their part that may have caused the other person's anger.

Some people, far from cooling things down for a moment and resuming the conversation later, forget that emotional ice cubes need to be removed. They continue to act cold and impassive for too long. Sometimes, they don't even remember the conflict that caused the estrangement. They only know that their ego was hurt and that they have to stand firm and maintain control of the relationship. This indifference may be due to the difficulty of finding a way to resolve the conflict on their own.

B) Causes that can lead to the application of the silent treatment

As a starting point, it is logical to think that the silent treatment is evidence of problems or emotional immaturity. When someone tries to create physical or emotional distance from another person with whom they have an emotional bond, they are actually revealing a problem. This shows that they have a **weakness** in their emotional relationships or **insecurity** about their own feelings. They find it difficult to form emotional bonds with other people. In short, they display **immaturity or emotional disability** that prevents them from having a healthy relationship based on communication and mutual affection.

In an abusive relationship (whether conscious or unconscious on the part of the abuser), the person who refuses to communicate usually postpones or tries to avoid it at all costs. Sometimes we see this as an attempt to buy time due to their own emotional insecurities, while other times it is used to avoid commitment and at the same time avoid ending the relationship and depriving themselves of what it brings them. They are undoubtedly trying to have the best of both worlds: a partner who loves them and goes out of their way for them, and emotional independence.

In any case, each person is unique, and the **reasons** why one person gives another the silent treatment can vary greatly and will always depend on the personality and intentions of the individual. Some causes are more "understandable" than others, since while sometimes we act this way unconsciously or by imitating what has been done to us, for example, during our childhood, other times it is done consciously, premeditatedly, and even pathologically and cruelly. Let's look at some of these causes:

- **Control of the relationship**: The person wants to impose when and how the subject is discussed and thus demonstrate who is in charge of the relationship.

- It is **emotional blackmail** to get the other person to submit to their desires and needs.

- **Seeking an apology:** The other person is manipulated and forced to acknowledge their mistakes and feel guilty. The cessation of communication seeks restitution or compensation from the other person, usually in the form of an apology that feeds the ego of the narcissist who thinks they are always right and that everyone has to accept them as they are.

- Desire for **punishment and revenge**: The aim is to hurt and strike back for something that is still resented.

- **Defense** mechanism **against fear of commitment**: They cannot stand the intensity of the other person and want to put emotional distance between them. They want to escape or avoid talking about their feelings, probably to avoid reaching an emotional commitment.

- **Insecurity or lack of emotional development**: The person is unable to identify, understand, and manage their own emotions in the face of conflict. In this way, they escape the situation by avoiding talking about it.

- **Blockages** due to failures in previous relationships: This is closely related to the previous cause, as this insecurity or lack of development has led to failures in other emotional relationships and/or vice versa.

- **Attention seeking:** Some people are so emotionally immature that they behave like children throwing tantrums. If something does not go their way, they rebel and shut down until they get attention and their wishes are fulfilled.

- **Pathological narcissistic interest**: pure interest in maintaining a relationship that benefits them (sexually or emotionally) and where they are in a position of power. These are literally people who emotionally "suck" the other person dry or simply use them for sex while not letting them leave because they know they are emotionally "hooked."

Silence as a weapon and shield

A person who suffers from silence or feels ignored in their demands or questions about the relationship can become depressed. Despite this, the person who practices this silence or distance will try to find a way to make the other person feel guilty about the situation. They will look for more or less valid reasons to justify their behavior. They will thus try to hide the real reasons for the emotional void they are subjecting the other person to.

These reasons always point to the victim as being guilty of having a wrong or different point of view. What's more, the latter may even set themselves up as the victim of possible harassment if the victim presses them to talk again and again. However, it cannot be harassment when the relationship continues freely. The victims of the silent treatment can easily fall into a process of destroying their own self-esteem. They may suffer from helplessness and severe emotional pain when they see that they always receive negative reinforcement.

A disguised form of psychological abuse

Basically, victims of this type of psychological abuse reach a point where they become accustomed to encountering a wall or emotional distance, which they are then accused of causing with their insistence. In these cases, if the relationship continues voluntarily on both sides, there is clearly a power imbalance where **emotional suffering** is inevitable. This type of behavior is very damaging to the other person. If someone we care about acts this way, a whole range of negative emotions will accompany us throughout the conflict. This conflict will be difficult to manage if there is a lack of dialogue and communication. In this way, the victim will become crazy, and the problem will grow bigger and bigger. As we can see, silence used with bad intentions is a very powerful weapon that aims to control, abuse, punish, and humiliate the other person.

CHAPTER 2

Who applies the silent treatment and why?

"Some people try to be tall by cutting off other people's heads."
—Paramahansa Yogananda

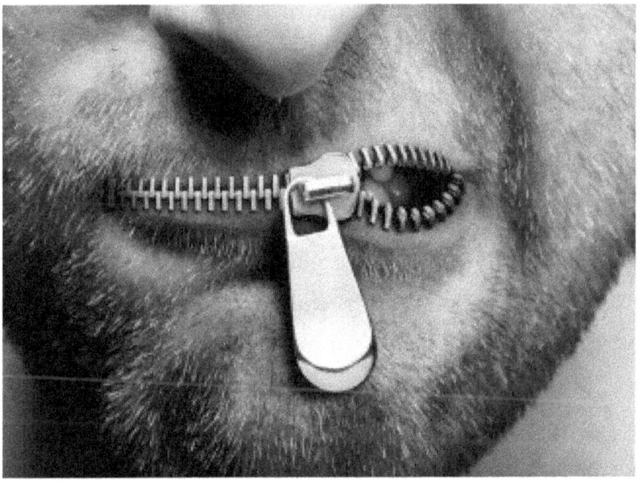

The silent treatment is a tactic widely used by people who appear to be **very rational** and have a high level of **self-control**. They are also characterized as **thoughtful** people who analyze and mull over a situation to find arguments that justify their **emotionally cold** behavior toward those who love them. But don't be fooled, the real problem lies elsewhere.

The type of people who use the silent treatment on others are often described by their victims as insensitive, manipulative, cold, calculating, convoluted, etc. They tend to have **hard emotional armor** that prevents them not only from falling in love or committing themselves or simply giving love, but also blocks other people from reaching them. For example, even though these people think they are in love with their partners, what they feel is an unhealthy attachment, a need for attention and submission. Their internal deficiencies prevent them from loving with respect, freedom, and mutual emotional independence. Later, we will explore how we can work on this.

The Inner World of Those Who Use Silence

The psychological profile of a person who habitually uses the silent treatment is often characterized by a combination of factors. They often have low self-esteem and a low tolerance for frustration and conflict. Their inability to manage their own emotions, especially negative ones such as anger or pain, leads them to resort to silence as a rudimentary tool of expression, as they lack the skills to communicate their needs assertively.

This behavior is, in many cases, a learned pattern. These individuals are likely to have grown up in family environments where silence was the usual method of dealing with disagreements or was used as a form of punishment by caregivers. Having been modeled as a "normal" response, they may use it in their adult relationships without being fully aware of its harmful nature or the existence of healthier alternatives.

In more severe cases, the silent treatment is a distinctive tactic of individuals with **narcissistic personality disorder (NPD)** or pronounced narcissistic traits. For them, silence is not a defense mechanism, but a calculated **"power move"** to punish, manipulate, and subdue their partner, thereby reaffirming their sense of grandiosity and control over the relationship. Attachment style also plays a role; the behavior is often linked to an avoidant attachment style, in which the person feels uncomfortable with emotional intimacy and withdraws during conflict as a form of self-protection from a perceived threat.

A) Understanding narcissistic abuse

In situations where the silent treatment is given repeatedly, the pattern of a person with pathological narcissistic traits and sometimes with a determined intention to cause harm is frequently present. These practices are directly related to the pathological narcissist:

- **Intolerance to criticism or rebuttal**: These are people who are used to not being contradicted and show an excessive attachment to their own ego based on a supposed superiority.

- **They constantly compare themselves** to others, which also leads them to compete in love. Their own insecurities lead them to want to appear and obtain the control they need to counteract those same emotional deficiencies. They think that if they control the relationship, they will not be hurt or suffer for love, and by controlling their partner, they ensure that the other person will not abandon them. The curious thing is that the silence with which they "punish" their partner is perceived as a threat of abandonment by the victim.

- **Abusive use of power** (in a couple or in any relationship): Once again, we return to the idea of the urgent need to impose one's will and control all situations and even the behavior of the other person.

- **Tendency to manipulate** to achieve goals

The Motivations Behind the Wall of Silence

Why does this type of person give someone the silent treatment if they supposedly love him/her? The reasons that drive someone to erect a wall of silence are varied, although they can be grouped into several main categories:

Control and Punishment: In the most abusive contexts, the primary motivation is to exercise power and control over the other person. By withdrawing communication, the abuser deliberately creates an atmosphere of anxiety, guilt, and uncertainty. This psychological tension is designed to drive the victim into a state of desperation where they are more likely to give in, apologize (even without knowing why), or comply with the aggressor's demands, all in order to end the painful silence. It is explicit punishment for a perceived transgression.

Conflict Avoidance: For others, silence is a shield. They use it as a defense mechanism to avoid confrontations they find frightening or overwhelming. They may fear their own anger, their partner's reaction, or the vulnerability that comes with expressing their true feelings. Although the intention is not to punish, this avoidance strategy is deeply dysfunctional, as it prevents problems from being resolved and corrodes the relationship from within.

Emotional Flooding: Sometimes silence is not a tactic, but a physiological shutdown. The person feels so distressed or emotionally overwhelmed that their ability to process information and respond verbally shuts down. The brain goes into a "freeze" state in response to acute stress. Although the impact on the victim is still harmful, the intention is not malicious manipulation, but a momentary inability to cope with the situation.

Dysfunctional Communication: Paradoxically, some people use silence as their only form of communication in times of conflict. It is a passive-aggressive signal of their unhappiness, pain, or anger when they lack the tools to express these emotions directly and assertively. They want their pain to be acknowledged, but they don't know how to ask for it, hoping that the other person will "guess" what is going on.

They don't want to lose you: The pattern that repeats itself in most cases is that, in the first place, giving you the silent treatment serves precisely that purpose, to not lose you, since they believe they have discovered a way to manipulate you and keep you by their side through fear of potential abandonment, which the silence is intended to anticipate.

They don't want to acknowledge their feelings or admit their emotional truth: Their huge narcissistic ego probably just enjoys seeing you submit to their manipulation and thus demonstrating their emotional power over you.

The use of the silent treatment presents a profound power paradox. It is behavior designed to establish dominance and control over another person, but at its core, it stems from an overwhelming feeling of internal powerlessness. The person who silences feels out of control on the inside—overwhelmed by emotions they cannot manage, plagued by insecurities, and fearful of conflict—and, as a result, attempts to exert tight control on the outside by manipulating their partner's reality and emotional state.

This understanding does not excuse abuse, but it reveals that aggression is also a symptom of the abuser's own deep-seated unresolved psychological issues, a key piece of information for any potential therapeutic intervention.

Exercising power to compensate for shortcomings

Like Gaslighting, this does not have to be malicious behavior; in many cases, it is poor communication combined with insecurities and defense mechanisms. But, again, this does not mean that they should not be held responsible, as it is they who decide to adopt this behavior to exercise control (to make the victim do what they want or change some behavior) or as a form of punishment. We are dealing with people who want to be in control (perhaps due to insecurities), lack empathy (or refuse to use it), or are emotionally immature and fear or do not know how to manage conflicts and their emotions (they avoid doing so).

It is also common for these people to seek **to take advantage of the other person's insecurities and fear of abandonment**. When they detect that they can exercise power over another person, this gives them security and strength in the face of their own insecurities and, in turn, guarantees that they will not be exposed to abandonment themselves, as they perceive the other person's level of commitment.

They are likely to refuse to talk about their insecurities or fears, let alone their traumas or emotional blocks. To do so, they usually need professional help. They are probably people who have **suffered emotional deprivation** at some point in their development or who have had difficult experiences in previous relationships. They do not want to go through the same thing again and, faced with this fear, prefer to anticipate possible events and always be in control of the relationship.

Another option that is quite common nowadays, and even more so in certain age groups where the percentage of separated or divorced people is higher, could be that the person **does not want an emotional involvement, only a sexual one** or other benefits for themselves.

What is a person with narcissistic personality disorder really like?

Narcissistic personality disorder occurs when someone has **excessive self-centeredness**. They believe they are better than others and deserve to always receive their attention and admiration. If you give them what they expect, you won't have any problems. However, if you fail to meet their expected quota of adoration, be prepared.

Narcissistic traits are not difficult to recognize, and in fact, many people who have them are not problematic. It is true that they behave selfishly, lack empathy, and are sometimes a bit exhibitionist. They are people who want to be the center of attention, be socially recognized, who often resist admitting their faults or lies, and who believe themselves to be extraordinary (even though their self-esteem, in some cases, is actually low).

Psychologist Stephen Johnson states that the narcissist is someone who has "buried their true self-expression in response to early injuries and replaced it with **a highly developed compensatory false** self." This alternative self often appears grandiose, "above others," and self-absorbed (154).

Numerous recent studies also claim that narcissism is on the rise worldwide, especially among young people. While narcissistic personality disorder remains a clinically diagnosed serious and fairly rare condition, subclinical narcissism or **narcissistic traits have reached**

epidemic proportions with serious consequences. Increasing levels of greed, self-obsession, superficial relationships, arrogance, and vanity are evident everywhere and are not making us happier, with common mental health problems on the rise, especially among young people. Seemingly irreversible disruptions to family life, technological developments, including social media, attitudes toward death, and the cult of the dying and celebrities are all part of the rise of our narcissistic society and are interconnected trends.

The **increase in people with narcissistic traits** may be due to many causes that we cannot address here due to lack of space, but among them we could point to: society's hyper-demanding nature in terms of personal achievement, the lack of adequate emotional education in the family, excessive concern about the personal image projected on social media, the work and personal environment, the growing problems of stress and depression caused by our fast-paced lives, and increased consumption of products and treatments (or *Vanity Capital)* to feel better and *selfie-proof.*

Experts point out that the younger generations have been raised as "narcissists" by parents who constantly tell them how special they are, overvaluing them and thus making them more vulnerable to failure and depression in the future. There is a tendency to confuse self-esteem with narcissism, when what needs to be cultivated is self-esteem, through love, support, attention, and boundaries.

According to Preston Ni, narcissism is correctly analyzed within a spectrum. This trait is normally distributed among the population, with most people remaining close to the middle and a few at the extremes. Healthy individuals who score slightly higher may be perceived as extremely charming, especially upon first meeting, but eventually reveal themselves to be vain. Such individuals may have uncomfortable or stressful personal encounters, but still have a fundamentally healthy personality (8).

We must recognize that a little narcissism is not bad, and in fact helps at certain stages of life, such as adolescence, when we need to establish our identity and personal value. Similarly, having an attractive personality and leadership skills is very positive and has nothing to do with narcissistic tendencies such as manipulation and deception. In the latter cases, it is highly recommended to quickly distance yourself from people with high levels of narcissism.

Narcissism does not necessarily represent an excess of self-esteem or insecurity, but rather a desire for appreciation or admiration, a need to be the center of attention, to feel unique. **The narcissist expects and desires special treatment** that reflects a supposed superiority over others. At the same time, it reflects a lack of empathy for others. If you encounter someone who consistently exhibits these behaviors, you may be dealing with a highly narcissistic individual.

What is the difference between narcissism and pathological narcissism?

Pathological narcissism, or narcissistic personality disorder, is rare, affecting around one percent of the population. The disorder is confirmed when narcissistic traits **affect a person's daily life and functioning.** This dysfunction usually causes conflict in relationships due to the pathological narcissist's lack of empathy and tendency to compete with others for attention. To feel superior, pathological narcissists often view everyone else as inferior, which makes them particularly intolerant of disagreement or criticism.

B) Narcissism in relationships

Narcissists almost always **make** a **good** first impression. A narcissistic person's desire to elicit admiration and praise, especially from potential romantic partners, often makes them charming and charismatic. The fact that they appear to have greater self-esteem than they actually do is something that most people appreciate and value. This arouses the interest and attraction of others and makes it easy for romance to blossom. However, their **inherent lack of empathy** sooner or later makes it difficult for them to understand the inner world of a partner and establish a satisfying long-term relationship.

But **can narcissists fall in love?** Narcissists can show a lot of passion and charm in the early stages of a relationship, just like anyone else who is fascinated by the attention they receive from someone they appreciate or are attracted to. Unfortunately, for most narcissists, relationships are purely transactions of energy that they need to survive. They provide positive attention and sexual satisfaction to reinforce their narcissistic ego and self-esteem with the goal of enjoying uncommitted pleasure. Most narcissists lose interest in the relationship when the expectation of intimacy or emotional commitment increases on the part of the other person, or they feel they have achieved the challenge of securing a relationship.

It is very difficult for people with narcissistic personality disorders to truly fall in love and build a healthy, equal relationship. These individuals often try to establish strict rules in a relationship regarding commitment/emotional freedom and even attempt to isolate a new partner from friends and family, among other disruptive behaviors.

The danger of unleashing narcissistic rage

In society in general, emotionally healthy people resolve their doubts, problems, and conflicts through communication. This is not the case when we talk about a narcissistic person. Generally, a narcissist gives us the silent treatment when what experts call **Narcissistic Rage**[1] is unleashed. Examples of narcissistic rage range from intense outbursts to passive-aggressive acts such as resentment, deliberate neglect, or cutting sarcasm, and of course, **the silent treatment.** What distinguishes narcissistic rage from normal anger is that it is usually irrational, disproportionate, and aggressive (or intensely passive-aggressive). This is because the narcissistic person's desires and whims are not being satisfied, which is a blow to their ego and idealized image of themselves.

---

1. **https://hijademadrenarcisista.wordpress.com/2019/10/28/la-ira-narcisista/**

Normally, some (or all) of the following scenarios trigger narcissistic anger, as we have already pointed out:

1. **Things do not go their way**, even when it is unreasonable. They are unable to properly manage the frustration this causes them.

2. **They are criticized** in some way, even when the criticism is diplomatic, reasonable, and constructive.

3. **They are not the center of attention**, and this bothers them, even when there are other priorities that justify it. As a result, they may take offense at something so minor that you didn't even notice it.

4. They are the ones who have broken a rule and **been "caught**."

5. They are required to take **responsibility** for what they have not done correctly. This angers them because it questions their worth and therefore damages their ego.

6. They do not receive **special treatment**, and this again represents an attack on their idealized or selfish self-image.

7. **They are accused** of manipulative behavior, exploitation, misrepresentation of information, etc.

8. The narcissist feels **threatened** by the possibility of losing control in their physical or relational environment.

In each of the above cases, narcissistic anger is used as a manipulative tool toward the outside world and as a device for avoiding pain within. Like a child throwing a tantrum because their wishes are not being fulfilled, the narcissist unleashes their "anger" to force their victims to give in to their desires. Ultimately, we will be upsetting them every time we do **something they don't like or consider inappropriate:** for example, not submitting to their will, setting limits, doing something contrary to what they were asking us to do, communicating our needs, sharing our ideas, feelings, and opinions. It scares them when the other person takes the initiative because they always want to be in control of the situation and the relationship.

Damaging the narcissistic ego is very dangerous and can have serious consequences depending on the emotional strength of the victim.

We stop feeding their ego when we make them feel inferior, either because we excel at something they know we are better at or simply because it reminds them of their shortcomings and flaws. As immature emotional beings, they feel attacked or abandoned when **they do not receive all the attention they need, or that they** want and expect.

Relationship Deterioration

The silent treatment is poison for any type of relationship, whether romantic, familial, or friendly. It directly attacks the foundations upon which a healthy connection is built.

Erosion of Trust: Trust, a fundamental pillar of intimacy, is systematically demolished. Silence creates an atmosphere of hostility, unpredictability, and emotional distance that makes it impossible to feel safe in the relationship.

Impossibility of Conflict Resolution: By blocking all communication, problems are prevented from being addressed and resolved. Unresolved grievances accumulate, generating resentment that becomes entrenched and poisons the dynamics of the relationship.

Demand-Withdrawal Cycle: The relationship often becomes trapped in a toxic demand-withdrawal cycle. One partner (the victim) desperately seeks connection and resolution, while the other (the aggressor) withdraws and entrenches in silence. This pattern is psychologically exhausting and inevitably leads to an irreparable emotional chasm between the two.

C) What is a narcissist really after with the silent treatment?

It is obvious that the common denominator in all cases is the need to boost their **low self-esteem** at the mere possibility of not being in control of the relationship. The narcissist applies the silent treatment when they are offended by something they see as criticism or by something you have said that they did not like, then they stop talking to you as a punishment to make you suffer. What they want to achieve by giving you the silent treatment is, apart from making you suffer, to confuse you and leave you wondering what you could have done wrong to make them do that to you. What they want is for you to react, beg them, and thus **mistreat you through emotional manipulation.** It is considered psychological abuse because it subjects the victim to recurring and premeditated emotional stress and suffering.[2] As French psychoanalyst Jean-Charles Bouchoux, author of *The Narcissistic Perverse,* states, "to cover up their problems, people with high levels of narcissism usually seek out one or two victims close to them. They don't need more than that, but they can make their lives miserable."

Internal destructive consequences of narcissistic anger

The narcissistic person is also a victim of their own pathology and behavior, as sooner or later they pay a high price for their "rage" and their narcissistic behavior in general. They often end up suffering from the following:

1. **Family estrangement** – Multiple studies have examined the relationship between narcissism and difficult family relationships.

2. **Breakups**: Narcissism also has negative repercussions on romantic relationships to the point of influencing the final outcome of divorces and relationship breakups. This is especially true because narcissists "use" people in some way rather than "relate" to them, and this is how they tend to leave behind many broken relationships. It is not surprising that they experience breakups with people who walk away after suffering the ravages of the narcissist and their manipulation, contempt, or deception.

3. **Loneliness and isolation** – Due to the above factors and despite being very sociable people, they tend to lead lonely lives precisely because they find it difficult to maintain and live with other people for long periods of time. Some narcissists achieve external success in life at the expense of others and feel lonely when they reach the top.

---

2. http://xn--vctima-3va.es/

5. **Missed opportunities** – When they find people who truly love them and are willing to help them improve, they are unable to overcome their own barriers to connecting in healthy relationships and making them last.

6. **Legal, financial, or professional problems** – They often come into conflict with many people, leading to rule-breaking, serious irresponsibility, and other legal actions against them or others.

7. **Damaged reputation** – Due to a lack of credibility, reliability, and personal and/or professional self-confidence.

8. **A deep fear of rejection** and of not being important – This is at the core of narcissistic rage. Many narcissists are constantly haunted by the insecurity that people may not see them as the privileged, powerful, popular, or "special" individuals they claim to be, and they react intensely when their fears are confirmed. Deep down, many narcissists feel like the "ugly duckling," even if they painfully refuse to admit it. See the references below.

Silence, a weapon for narcissists

Silence is a powerful weapon that, in the hands of a narcissist, can be used to manipulate others around them. When the narcissist realizes that we need their presence and communication, that's when they start to reduce the frequency with which they interact. They always do this with full use of their reasoning, and with the intention of **causing addiction using intermittent reinforcement.** If they are a narcissistic psychopath and realize that we want more than physical contact, they will begin to sporadically distance themselves and limit intimacy. If the narcissistic psychopath detects that we want their presence, they will add longer and longer silences.

Their world is ruled by power and control, and for these people, life is a simple game where there are only winners and losers. Their main goal is to win at any cost, there are no limits to how they act, and that puts others in serious danger. The narcissistic psychopath enjoys feeling loved.

Their self-esteem is so low that the only way to reinforce their value is by feeling loved, continuously.

They know they can manipulate their victim by hiding what they love most. Their innate ability to shut themselves off for hours, days, or even weeks makes them feel that **"we love them,"** and that is what gives them the energy they want to feel valued.

For a narcissistic psychopath, this is their main source of energy, and they can do this with several victims at once. It is not uncommon to find a narcissistic psychopath who has several relationships, in addition to their partner, creating the same type of situation with all of them.

In severe cases of narcissistic pathology, their lack of awareness allows them to destroy the lives of their victims without feeling any remorse. This is the basis of intermittent reinforcement and by giving the silent treatment, **they make their victim addicted** to them. It is a normal biological reaction that we cannot avoid, as we do not know that we are being manipulated.

If the narcissistic psychopath feels uncomfortable with a comment or an opinion that upsets them, they may start to apply **the "silent treatment"** because they cannot allow themselves to lose control. If someone comes to them with a request to balance the relationship or reach an agreement, they will take it as a threat to their controlled world, their fragile and flimsy integrity.

If we ask for more time together, more intimacy, or for them to modify some behavior that we find excessive to improve the relationship, they will punish us with **the silent treatment,** falling into an overwhelming silence. The victim then realizes that any attempt to improve the relationship will be punished with silence. This condemns the relationship to inevitable deterioration. And that is the psychopath's goal: to keep the victim in a perpetual state of confusion and uncertainty.

Consequences of giving the silent treatment:

The effects of the silent treatment are many and varied, depending on the victim's personality and emotional strength. Later on, we will see that people who are often victims of this behavior are themselves lacking in emotional resources for internal management and fundamentally have problems with self-esteem or emotional dependence (excessive attachment).

As we have been discussing, **abuse is not only about insults, shouting, hitting**, threats, or aggressive tones; making another person feel that they do not exist is also abuse. It is undoubtedly a covert or disguised passive-aggressive behavior. We can provoke negative or positive feelings in another person, and they will react according to those feelings. However, indifference towards someone suggests that there are no feelings, and this causes the victim a great deal of anxiety, pain, despair, and fear of breaking the bond that unites them. Some of the devastating effects of the silent treatment are as follows:

- **Emotional stress and trauma**: Ignoring someone can cause them to experience very intense negative feelings of devaluation and misunderstanding because they do not know how to interpret the reason for the silence. Being ignored by a family member, friend, or partner can be really painful. Obviously, the stronger the emotional bond, the greater the suffering and stress we will experience.

-**Feelings of sadness and/or depression:** When you ignore someone, you are implicitly and directly accusing them. For that person, the relationship becomes toxic and painful. Ignoring someone is an attack that hurts us deeply and causes resentment. Resentment builds up and sooner or later explodes, with consequences for our overall health.

-**Feelings of anger, fear, and guilt:** These feelings are due to the distress of not knowing what is causing the situation or what is being done wrong. In addition, when we are not taken into account, we experience feelings of helplessness.

-**Psychological stress:** Along with the emotional roller coaster described above, not only is self-esteem and self-worth destroyed, but there are also increases in stress levels, leading to sadness, loss, confusion, and abandonment, with the victim feeling that they have no control over the situation.

-Changes in the brain: According to the latest studies, the silent treatment can cause changes in the brain, specifically in the anterior cingulate cortex, whose function is to detect different pain thresholds in humans. Being excluded and ignored activates this area of the brain when someone is subjected to the silent treatment. When someone refuses to acknowledge the existence of their partner, child, etc. for hours, days, or weeks, it makes them feel as if they are somehow less than human, like a ghost.

- **Suicidal impulses**: The power of silence is very strong and aggressive, as it generates guilt, self-doubt, and a desire to escape the situation. Silence and indifference send us the message that we are not important, valuable, or worthy of attention.

CHAPTER 3

What is the victim of the silent treatment like?

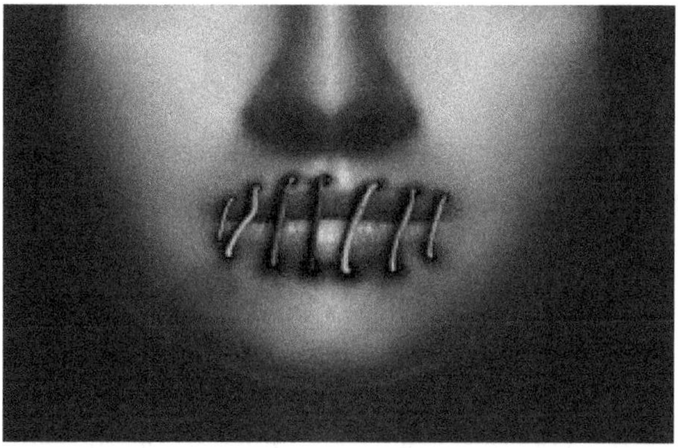

If you have ever recognized yourself as a victim of the silent treatment, it is highly recommended that you reflect on how you got into that situation and what there is about your personality or the way you relate to others that may have attracted this type of person. If you are still in the early stages, it is a good idea to explore what this abuse is like and analyze your tools to avoid it.

The torture inflicted on victims of a narcissistic psychopath with **the "silent treatment"** is terrible, and the damage caused in a relationship of this kind can take a long time to reverse for the victim. In the victim's mind, there is the idea that **by "changing"** certain behaviors, the relationship could be saved, and that is where their energy becomes blocked, without realizing that this is impossible. The narcissistic psychopath is not who you think they are, but a completely different being, with different laws and rules.

Narcissistic psychopaths take advantage of their victims' vulnerabilities. If the victim begins to get to know themselves and learn what their vulnerabilities are and reinforces them, that is when the psychopath will no longer be able to access them. If the victim notices that their attempts to improve the situation are met with silence from the other party, they must be assertive and direct. You cannot allow your attempts to be taken as rejection by the other party.

Express how you feel; your voice is the key to moving forward, overcoming emotional excess, and finding your place in the relationship. If the other party does not accept your place, then **you must make decisions.**

To begin with, you must **recognize whether you are emotionally dependent**, whether you have sufficient self-esteem, and whether these factors have led you into a toxic relationship. Being ignored is a very humiliating way to make the other person feel bad. Although you may think it is easy to overcome this situation, sometimes when it goes on for a long time and becomes an "emotional habit," the victim becomes accustomed to depending on the approval of the abuser to feel worthwhile and good about themselves. This is clear evidence of weakness on the part of the victim.

Factors of Vulnerability

Although the silent treatment is harmful to anyone, certain people are especially vulnerable to its effects. Individuals with high sensitivity to rejection, a history of trauma, or emotional neglect in childhood, may experience silence in a devastating way. For them, present-moment silence triggers deeply rooted fears of abandonment and reinforces core beliefs of being unworthy of love or fundamentally flawed. Similarly, people with an **anxious attachment style** may panic in the face of silence, leading them to plead, beg, or humiliate themselves to reestablish connection. Unfortunately, this is a reaction that reinforces the abuser's tactic by demonstrating its effectiveness.

The true cruelty of the silent treatment lies in the fact that it is a form of **"aggression by subtraction."** Unlike overt abuse, which adds trauma (an insult, a blow), the silent treatment works by removing fundamental human needs: connection, recognition, validation. This creates a psychological void that the victim's mind rushes to fill. Without receiving an external explanation for the silence, the brain turns inward in search of a cause, a process that almost invariably leads to self-blame: "What did I do wrong?" In this way, the abuser externalizes the dirty work of abuse to the victim's own mind. They simply create the conditions (silence), and the victim's psychological need to find a cause and restore connection does the rest, generating the anxiety, guilt, and doubt that the abuser desires.

A) Emotional dependence

From the moment we are born, human beings need to establish emotional connections with our emotional environment. This need increases as we grow up and remains with us for the rest of our lives. With the recognition and emotional support of others, we build our own identity. When the person next to us give us the "silent treatment," that is, ignores us or does not speak to us despite continuing to live in the same space, the emotional foundations on which we stand may begin to shake.

If the person being abused by their partner, children, or those closest to them experiences these situations frequently, they begin to feel helpless and empty, which ends up destroying them psychologically and emotionally. They begin to believe that they are not worthy of the attention, affection, and respect of others and suffer from

- Unhealthy attachment and emotional dependence
- Frustration
- Low self-esteem
- Confusion
- Self-blame
- Misunderstanding
- Depression

People who try to end the silent treatment by trying to win over the other person without success end up feeling even more hurt. There comes a time when you have to say to yourself, "I've done everything I can, and now I need to take care of myself so I don't get tortured by this." If this is the case, experts recommend seeking help in couples therapy and evaluating the future of the relationship if it becomes a toxic and repetitive pattern.

B) Self-esteem

"But do you love me?" asked Alice.
"No, I don't love you!" replied the White Rabbit.
Alice frowned and began to rub her hands, as she always did when she felt hurt.
"See?" said the White Rabbit. "Now you're wondering what you did wrong, why I can't love you at least a little, what makes you so imperfect, so fragmented. That's why I can't love you.
Because there will be days when I'll be tired, angry, with my head in the clouds, and I'll hurt you. Every day we trample on feelings out of boredom, carelessness, and misunderstanding. But if you don't love yourself at least a little, if you don't create a shield of pure joy around your heart, my weak darts will become lethal and destroy you. The first time I saw you, I made a pact with myself: "I will avoid loving you until you have learned to love yourself."
That's why, Alicia, no, I don't love you.
I can't do it.
-Alice in Wonderland- Lewis Carrol

Sometimes we need to ask ourselves why we are a recurring victim of abusive behavior such as the silent treatment. It is obvious that a narcissist knows very well how to choose their victims and find their weaknesses to manipulate them. Therefore, if this is your case, it is important that you reflect alone on your self-perception. In other words, review your self-esteem. Anyone in a normal life can have certain difficulties. If they do not solve them, either because they do not face them or because they do so in the wrong way, their self-esteem is likely to suffer. In other words, self-esteem could be understood more as a consequence or effect of problems than as a cause of them. Often when people complain about their bad luck or how bad things are going, they blame something external (they don't have low self-esteem) or themselves (low self-esteem).

What do we hide behind "low self-esteem"? Fear. Sometimes we are afraid to face situations because they paralyze us, and we think we must act in one way or another when sometimes we just must accept what is happening to us because it is not up to us. There is a type of self-esteem called **"contingent self-esteem based on relationships"** because, as probably happened to us in childhood, we depend on the positive reactions of loved ones to feel good about ourselves. Our value depends on constant signs of approval, which is why we constantly seek positive reinforcement of the love we are given.

How can you tell if you are in a relationship because of low self-esteem?

You tend to "put up with things" and are accommodating and even submissive because you think that your partner will love you more that way. A 2015 study by Dr. Megan McCarthy at the University of Waterloo says that when you are in a romantic relationship and have low self-esteem:

— You silence your own needs so as not to "upset" the other person.

— There is a tendency to resort to emotional blackmail rather than talking about problems directly.

— You are hypervigilant about everything your partner does or says.

— Everything has a double meaning for you, and you interpret "signals" based on your fears.

– You live with insecurity about your relationship or your partner's love.

– You take every suggestion as criticism and criticism as tragedy.

– You become paranoid or jealous.

– You are neither happy nor at peace.

– The possibility of the relationship ending terrifies you and affects your health. You perceive it as ingratitude or abandonment. You feel that you cannot live without your partner. Because you are left without someone who reflects you back to yourself, which means that without that person, you "no longer exist" or your life no longer has purpose. You have anxiety attacks, depression, sleep disturbances, appetite disturbances, and you gain or lose weight significantly.

According to Walter Riso, an expert in emotional dependence, the four pillars and components that make up self-esteem are **self-concept**, **self-image**, **self-reinforcement**, and **self-efficacy**. Here are some techniques and exercises to help you start working on your self-esteem and self-awareness.

C) Self-awareness: First, get to know yourself. Talk to yourself.

Self-awareness is a reflective process in which a person gains an understanding of themselves, what characterizes them, their qualities and flaws, their limitations, needs, hobbies, and fears. It is a preliminary step in understanding and making sense of life and everything around us. Ask yourself *"why?"* about your fears, for example. Reflect on your values.

What makes you happy? How would you like to be/what would you like to do in 10, 20, or 30 years? Of everything you know or have learned, what is important or what have you discovered through experience and your relationships? What happens around you or inside you when you feel happy? What kind of life do you want to have? How do you like to imagine yourself in 10, 20 or 30 years?

Take action, don't be afraid of failure

Human beings tend to avoid and not face what they fear and what causes them anxiety, as this eliminates the anxiety that the situation causes. However, the main enemy of **low self-esteem** is simply doing nothing. It has been proven that self-esteem does not depend on the outcome of your actions. It simply depends on whether you act. In this way, self-esteem increases when you face circumstances and decreases when you avoid them. If you act and achieve positive results, the reinforcement is obvious, but even when you fail, you gain useful life lessons that will make you wiser next time. There are no failures, only lessons.

Replace your goals with values

Sometimes, not achieving highly specific and desired goals can lead to frustration and feelings of worthlessness. However, if it is values rather than goals that guide us in life, this will not happen. For example, imagine that you are preparing for a competitive exam and have been studying for months. In this case, your values are effort, perseverance, self-improvement, sacrifice, and willpower. If you ultimately fail the exam and don't get the job, the values you have upheld during this stage of your life will always be there to make you feel very proud of yourself.

Identify your strengths

Today we know that each and every one of us is born with a set of qualities, innate characteristics, or strengths that are our strong points. These are the skills you are particularly good at. The problem arises when a person with **low self-esteem** does not believe they have these strengths and also finds it very difficult to identify them.

Practice this exercise:

1. Think of five achievements you have accomplished in your life: finishing your degree, working in the sector you wanted to work in, learning a third language, playing a musical instrument, learning to cook on your own, seducing your partner... If you find it difficult to come up with any, it's because you're not being generous with yourself, so imagine that a friend had achieved that success. What would you say to them? How would you acknowledge them? Then think **about what positive personal characteristics** are necessary to achieve each of those accomplishments, and you will recognize your strengths.

Another very interesting exercise is to write a letter to yourself describing yourself in the third person. Then continue describing yourself in the third person as if the letter were written by someone who loves you very much. *What I like most about him/her is that... Some of the people who love him/her most are... What he/she is most proud of is... What he/she would need to feel more comfortable with himself/herself and have more self-esteem is to stop...*

Turn your negative thoughts into rational responses

Our internal dialogue is fundamental in building our self-esteem. In people with healthy self-esteem, this dialogue is usually kind, positive, and comforting. But in people with **low self-esteem**, it becomes the opposite, with a voice that constantly criticizes, punishes, and belittles their achievements. This inner voice is irrational and tends to interpret any situation in the worst possible way, even when there is no objective evidence to reach that conclusion.

What should we do? Identify those irrational, negative thoughts about yourself and question their objectivity, replacing them with more realistic and objective ones. You will have to put them to the test so that your reason can overcome them. Is it a real threat or is it completely unfounded? Identify in which situations they appear and what exactly they say to you. Your negative thoughts are usually always the same, so how do they make you interpret situations? What emotions do they provoke in you? The better you understand the emotions they cause, the less power they will have over you, because recognizing the emotion you feel reduces its impact.

Separate yourself from your fears

When fear arises, don't ignore it or block it out. Acknowledge it, greet it, and immediately say goodbye! It's important to understand that we are not what we think, and that when we think about something, it doesn't mean it's going to happen. Our minds love to bombard us with negative thoughts, and your job is to stop identifying with them. That way, they will lose all their power. Imagine a stream of water carrying leaves. Visualize your fear on top of a leaf as the river carries it away and it slowly disappears. It will take practice at first, but with time you will get there.

Forgive yourself, practice self-compassion.

To improve self-esteem, it is essential to learn not to be overly hard on ourselves and to forgive ourselves for our mistakes. Self-compassion is closely related to self-concept (one of the four elements that make up self-esteem) and consists of treating yourself with the same empathy you would treat your best friend. That is, giving yourself support and being understanding with yourself, rather than constantly criticizing and judging yourself. It involves learning to calm yourself down and comfort yourself so you can try again, rather than punishing yourself every time you make a mistake.

There are many **exercises** and **activities** to develop self-compassion, but the simplest is to talk to yourself the way you would talk to a friend who is going through a difficult time. This way, you will begin to see your problems as something you are experiencing, rather than something that defines you. Would you tell a friend that they are useless or incapable of doing anything right? Probably not, right? So every time you catch yourself punishing yourself, replace your critical voice with compassionate **phrases**. Your self-esteem will thank you for it.

Stand up straight and smile

Nonverbal body language influences our mood, and to counteract this, it is a good practice to "cheer ourselves up" with beneficial postures such as standing up straight and expansively when we are sad or down, or simply trying to smile and think about positive things around us. These types of poses (head up, shoulders back, and hands on hips) are called power poses, and it has been shown that holding them for just two minutes is enough to boost your confidence, make you feel better, and feel more self-assured.

Exercise

Exercise increases self-esteem in the short term, and thirty minutes of moderate aerobic exercise a day is enough to reduce cortisol levels and increase your well-being thanks to the release of endorphins.

CHAPTER 4

Tips and guidelines for dealing with the silent treatment

Whether we are on one side of the coin or the other, we must be aware that the silent treatment is not a good way to manage conflict and can create a lot of tension and resentment between people. Ignoring someone in order to upset or punish them can be a weapon that can damage a person's self-esteem, self-image, and even their identity. It is not an educational tool. Giving the silent treatment is not as subtle or insignificant as it may seem, but rather a form of psychological abuse and mistreatment in disguise that you need to be aware of and informed about.

Furthermore, navigating a relationship with a narcissist can be deeply frustrating and distressing. In their quest for control and admiration, narcissists can manipulate and exploit others, damaging their self-esteem and even aiming to alter their sense of reality. Arguing with a narcissist about their actions is often futile, and the most effective solution is to set boundaries and distance yourself emotionally. You may not be able to control your feelings for someone, but you can control how you respond to them. Cutting ties with a narcissistic partner or family member may be the best, if not the only, solution. If you are the one giving the silent treatment, take note of the tips and guidelines below and try to reflect on them.

A) If you are a victim of the Silent treatment:

Being on the receiving end of the silent treatment can make you feel invisible and manipulated. But what are some strategies for dealing with a narcissist? Recognizing your frustration, appreciating where the behavior is coming from, and refusing to lose your own sense of purpose when a narcissist takes center stage are some key strategies. The silent treatment causes confusion in the person receiving it. When they can't find explanations, they feel anxious and then guilty. It's a form of invisible violence that stems from a passive-aggressive game.

Healthily managing the silent treatment in a relationship

If the problem arose because one or both of you have trouble communicating your emotions effectively, it is best **to practice active listening**, try to understand what the other person is trying to express, and signal that you are really listening attentively. For example, remain silent while listening without interrupting and looking at the other person, nod your head, use expressions such as "I see, I understand," or ask questions. All of this helps to connect with the desire of all human beings to be heard and understood.

Another fundamental aspect is **to practice self-control** so that the other person's words do not affect you when deciding what to say or not to say. **Try listening to the other person** for at least five minutes and breathe slowly, seeking calm within yourself if something they say upsets you at any point.

Finally, distance occurs because **resentment has built up between the two of you.** If resentment has not been properly dealt with for a long time, it is time to **forgive**, to stop blaming or blaming yourself for the past that cannot be changed.

Practice empathy whenever you can: There is an important reflection that few people make when they only see reasons to be angry: How might our partner be experiencing the relationship? What is going through their head or heart when they say this or that? How do they feel?

Remember that in emotional relationships, it is normal for there to be no good guys or bad guys (except in the case of sick psychopaths). It's not a matter of settling scores, but of taking a new dual perspective, yours and the other person's. Forgiveness and the desire for change are carried out for the greater good, which is to enjoy the power of growth and well-being that a healthy relationship gives us.

Some tips for breaking the silence

– **Give them** enough **time** to calm down after an argument. Half a day is more than enough. Write down that you want to talk and leave it where they can see it when they are alone.

– Ask them to sit down and talk while you share breakfast or a snack. If you have difficulty expressing your feelings and emotions, you can always seek professional counseling and help to teach you how to communicate better and more assertively.

– **Speak with love and respect**. Reconnecting with the emotional warmth you once felt depends on the cause of the rift between you, but above all, on your determination to break the ice.

– **Be patient** if they don't want to sit down at first.

– **Be assertive** and stand up for your rights. Don't show anger or force the person to talk to you in a passive-aggressive way, and don't provoke an argument. Give each other some space until the situation calms down, and try to appear relaxed and positive. This will help you get closer to each other.

– **Avoid isolating yourself:** maintaining relationships with family, friends, neighbors, and coworkers will make it easier to weather your partner's mood swings.

– **Maintain a rich inner life:** Participating in hobbies, reading, and art projects can help you stay strong and stable while dealing with your partner's silent hostility.

– **Remember yourself:** One of the problems with being in a relationship with an abusive and controlling partner is that it can be difficult to remember who you are. This is known as perspecticide. Don't let your opinions, desires, and goals be erased.

– **Seek professional counseling:** A therapist who understands control and abuse can help you understand what has happened and face the challenges ahead.

– **Decide on your boundaries:** Recognize that the silent treatment is just one tactic in the toolbox of someone who controls your relationship. Decide what your boundaries are. That is the way to live according to your personal values. If you feel that the situation is harmful to you or family members, seek help and find a safe way out of the relationship.

– **Consider ending the relationship if there is no other remedy:** you do not need to stay in a relationship where your partner is mean or cruel to you, whether through the silent treatment, verbal, physical, or sexual abuse, financial control, or any other means. If the situation becomes untenable, you must act as you would when facing an iceberg in the distance. Do not let it sink you; run to save yourself before the Titanic sinks.

Focus on yourself

Identify your role during the silent treatment. Once you have gained some space for yourself, you can use this time to consider how to interpret the other person's silence. This does not mean that you should blame yourself, but rather empower yourself to recognize and change the communication patterns that may have led you to this point.

As you reflect on your interactions with that person, try to find common patterns in your own behavior. For example, your boyfriend was talking to you and you interrupted him because you assumed you knew what he was about to say. If he then went silent, your tendency to "predict" his thoughts could cause him frustration and make him pull away. Listen actively to avoid causing the silent treatment in this type of situation. Don't interrupt your partner when they are speaking. Give them time to express their message completely before responding.

Reduce anger to avoid escalating the situation. Feeling manipulated can cause anger, which can push an unhelpful interaction into dangerous territory. Recognize that displaying anger will not be productive for your relationship. Use the space you get during the silent treatment to mitigate any negative emotions you are feeling. Try some relaxation techniques, such as guided meditations, deep breathing, progressive muscle relaxation, or gentle stretching to reduce anger and promote calm. If you need time to cool down, try taking an hour-long break or even agree to reschedule the conversation for the next day, but don't put it off for too long.

Set personal boundaries. When you set effective boundaries in your relationships, you increase the likelihood that you will live according to your values. Whether the person giving you the silent treatment is a parent, friend, or partner, you can set personal boundaries to prevent a toxic pattern in the relationship from hurting your feelings.

First, think about how you want to be treated in your relationships and what you will and won't accept from those around you to set boundaries. Once you've established boundaries, share these expectations with your loved ones. Keep in mind that if you've been emotionally abused in the past, you may feel confused about how you should be treated in relationships. For example, you could say, "I care about you and enjoy spending time with you. However, when you suddenly stop talking to me, it makes me feel confused and powerless. If you continue to act this way, I will have to distance myself from you to protect my own emotional health and well-being."

Take care of yourself. Even if the other person wants to hurt you, don't beat yourself up when you're alone for being a victim of the situation. Distract yourself by doing things that relax you and make you smile to counteract the negative effects of the silent treatment. Exercise, go for a walk, call a friend to chat, light a candle, and take a bubble bath. These are all excellent ideas for taking care of yourself and improving your mental health during the silent treatment.

Dealing with a narcissist's silent treatment

If the silent treatment is a chronic behavior pattern in the person you are dealing with, we have already seen that this person may have narcissistic traits. Being in a relationship with a narcissist can be emotionally exhausting and confusing. However, there are some strategies you can use to improve your interactions with that person. If you must interact with the narcissist (because at that moment there is no other choice), it is important:

1. **Don't react.** Remember that any action a narcissist takes to hurt us is done with the intention of getting something from us, such as narcissistic fuel. If we don't react, we will destabilize them. Not reacting means not responding, not asking questions, not seeking them out, not trying to "fix" things, and not demanding attention.
2. **Take control when the narcissist resumes communication.** When narcissists decide unilaterally to talk to you again, they will do so as if nothing had happened. It is their way of feeling that they have the power and that they do things when they want and how they want. Tell them you need time to think. That you will talk to the narcissist when you feel it is appropriate. Then, apply **zero contact.** Don't tell them how long you need to respond. Put them on hold just like the narcissist put you on hold.
3. **Set your own boundaries** and tell them (always speaking in the first person and calmly) that you will not tolerate that kind of behavior. Don't expect a dialogue; dialogue with a narcissist is impossible.
4. **Never beg for love.** Far from moving them, it feeds their ego.
5. **Don't apologize for something you didn't do.** Don't agree with them if they're wrong.
6. **Don't pressure them to talk constantly.** This will only make their reactions worse. Don't try to force things. Give them a few hours and then send them a message letting them know that you know they're angry. Invite them to talk and let them know that you're willing to listen.
7. **Don't show how hurt you are,** either in their presence or through other people or on social media. That's exactly what they want, to see you suffer, so don't give them the satisfaction of getting their way. Avoid showing any reaction. Although some people use the silent treatment without realizing the toxic

effects it has on relationships, others intentionally distance themselves and ignore you in order to hurt your feelings.

In either case, if you start apologizing (even if you don't know what you did wrong) or begging the person to pay attention to you, you're feeding the beast. Instead, consider the silent treatment as a pass to reflect. Don't show anger, don't passively or aggressively force the person to talk to you, and don't provoke an argument. Just give them and yourself some space until things calm down.

1. **Adopt healthier communication styles**, take care of yourself instead of obsessing over the other person, and identify and stop the emotional abuse to regain your power in this situation.
2. **Zero contact:** If you have no need or obligation to interact with the narcissist, zero contact is not only healing, but also liberating. There comes a time in the life of every victim (whether from a narcissistic family or any other similar relationship) when we have two choices:

1. Stay within the family environment, putting our physical, emotional, and mental health at risk (in some cases, even our own life is at risk).

2. Cut all harmful ties through physical and emotional distance and by applying **zero contact.**

Starting to apply zero contact is not an easy task. It requires a lot of courage, being firm with the decision made, and not backing down. Narcissistic abusers have previously programmed us to give in to their blackmail and manipulation (through fear and guilt). In addition, they create **cognitive dissonance** in the victim by alternating periods of affection with periods of devaluation and abuse.

Mindfulness and self-compassion: tools for victim healing

Recovery from emotional abuse, and in particular from the silent treatment, is a process that requires rebuilding the internal security and sense of worth that have been eroded. Mindfulness and self-compassion are evidence-based practices that offer a powerful set of therapeutic tools for healing these wounds.

Mindfulness is the practice of paying attention to the present moment in a deliberate and nonjudgmental way. For a victim of emotional abuse, whose nervous system may be in a constant state of alert, this practice is a way to break out of the cycle of anxious thoughts about the past (what I did wrong) and the future (when it will happen again). The goal is not to suppress thoughts or emotions, but to learn to observe them as passing mental events without getting caught up in them. This creates a crucial space between the stimulus (the abuser's silence) and the automatic reaction (anxiety, panic, self-blame), giving the person back a sense of control over their internal state.

Fundamental practices include:

- **Mindful breathing:** This is the most basic and accessible practice. It simply involves focusing your attention on the physical sensation of breathing—the air entering and leaving your nostrils, the rising and falling of your abdomen. This act anchors you in the present and has a direct calming effect on the nervous system.
- **Body scan:** This meditation involves directing your attention sequentially to different parts of your body, noticing any sensations (heat, tingling, tension, neutrality) without judging them. It is a powerful technique for releasing physical tension where trauma is often stored and for reconnecting the mind with the body, from which the victim may have dissociated as a defense mechanism.
- **Mindful observation:** This involves using the five senses to connect with the immediate environment. It can be as simple as

carefully observing a leaf, listening to ambient sounds without labeling them, or savoring a cup of tea, paying attention to its aroma, warmth, and taste. This takes the mind out of the rumination loop and anchors it in the tangible reality of the present moment.

Guided meditations and visualizations to rebuild inner security

For those new to these practices or whose nervous system is particularly dysregulated by trauma, guided meditation is an invaluable resource. They offer a structure and a reassuring voice that guides the person through the process of relaxation and healing.

Creating a safe space: A highly effective visualization technique involves creating an imaginary **"safe place."** The person is guided to mentally construct a space (real or fantastical) where they feel completely safe, calm, and protected. This internal sanctuary becomes a resource they can return to at any time of distress to find comfort and stability.

Use of affirmations: Affirmations are positive statements that are repeated to challenge and reprogram negative beliefs internalized as a result of abuse. For victims of the silent treatment, affirmations such as "I am worthy of love and respect," "My feelings are valid," "I have the right to be heard," or "My value does not depend on the approval of others" are essential for rebuilding self-esteem and reclaiming personal power.

The healing power of self-compassion

Self-compassion is the practice of treating oneself with the same kindness, care, and understanding that one would offer a good friend who is suffering. It is the direct antidote to the shame, guilt, and self-criticism that fuel emotional abuse. Self-compassion consists of three interrelated components:

- **Self-Kindness:** This involves being gentle and understanding with oneself in times of pain or failure, rather than being harshly self-critical.

- **Common humanity:** This is the recognition that suffering, imperfection, and failure are part of the shared human experience. This combats feelings of isolation and the belief that "this only happens to me."
- **Mindfulness:** Consists of keeping painful thoughts and emotions in a balanced awareness, without ignoring them but without getting carried away by them.

Practical exercises to cultivate self-compassion:

- **Write a compassionate letter:** Write a letter to yourself from the perspective of an unconditionally loving friend, acknowledging your pain, validating your feelings, and offering words of encouragement and support.
- **Positive self-talk:** Consciously interrupt the flow of self-criticism and replace it with compassionate language. A key question to ask yourself is, "What would I say to a friend in this same situation?"
- **Gestures of comfort:** The body responds to physical gestures. Simple acts such as placing a hand on your heart, stroking your arm, or giving yourself a hug can activate the body's calming system and release oxytocin, promoting feelings of safety and well-being.

These practices are not mere passive coping mechanisms. They are active forms of neurological and psychological resistance against the effects of abuse. The silent treatment works by disrupting the victim's nervous system and attacking their self-esteem. Mindfulness practices directly counteract the physiological stress response, while self-compassion actively combats cognitive damage, replacing the internalized voice of the abuser with one of kindness and validation. In this way, healing is transformed from a passive wait to an active and empowering journey of personal reconstruction.

How do narcissists react when we apply zero contact?

Badly, very badly. A narcissist never wants to lose and will never take NO for an answer. As it is impossible to have a dialogue, it is often not even necessary to warn them that we have decided to cut off all communication. Remember that such an action activates the **narcissistic wound**, triggering a reaction of **anger** on the part of the narcissist. Sometimes, in order to protect our integrity, it is necessary to simply walk away.

What will the narcissist try when we apply zero contact?

As narcissists are people with an inflated ego, they will try by any means to break the zero contact. They will start with their tactics of blackmail, manipulation, coercion, threats, etc. to break us down emotionally and psychologically and thus get what they want.

B) If you are the one giving the Silent treatment:

"Love is not enough for a relationship to work."

If you recognize yourself in the above description of the type of person who applies the silent treatment, how they do it, and its consequences, I hope you are reflecting on the need to acknowledge the problem and make a decision to change.

Psychologist Escalpez points out that many people act this way unconsciously, "probably **conditioned by their existential baggage**." Generally, they are also unaware of the suffering their behavior causes. If this is your case, don't beat yourself up, but make a firm resolution to learn to manage your emotions differently and to recognize that this is an abusive practice.

Understanding the harm it causes is the first step to resolving it. Silence or indifference is not the solution to any problem, and using them as "punishment" does not lead to anything good. Think that the person you love should stay by your side because you treat them well and they are happy with you.

If you are someone who exhibits these behaviors, consider your willingness to change and improve the situation. Keep in mind that according to experts, there are two types of abusers. On the one hand, there are **psychopaths**, who are very intelligent and do what they do out of pure selfishness and because they believe they benefit from the abuse.

In this case, **treatment is difficult** due to the risk of recurrence. On the other hand, there are those who do it out of **insecurity,** because they don't know how to relate to others, have **little control over their impulses,** and/or have not had healthy role models to look up to throughout their lives. In these cases, **they do tend** to **improve** with therapy, which is often very helpful for them.

Often, the worst aspects of people come to the surface with those closest to them, and this can cause a lot of damage, whether to family, friends, or partners. If we are aware that we have this type of behavior, someone will point it out to us, or we will simply notice that someone close to us is suffering because of how we behave towards them. If we are unable to correct it, we should give therapy a try. Behaving in a toxic way not only damages those around you by undermining your relationships, but also damages yourself.

You are not necessarily a toxic person at heart, but what is toxic is the way you have learned to communicate and manage your emotions. When there is no clear communication and the other person is manipulated, this does not lead to conflict resolution, but rather to the deterioration of relationships. You are not always going to have power, control, or authority over others, nor is it a good thing. People do not want to live with someone who always wants to impose their will on them. In the end, you know that you can end up in a very deep loneliness.

Try to remember and **identify where you learned to act or react this way** and remember how you felt when it happened. Try to say what is bothering you without getting upset or simply say how you feel about something that has happened instead of acting with silence. Life and relationships are not a game of gestures and silence. If you don't speak because you think "you can't talk to the other person," the truth is probably that you don't like hearing what the other person has to say. That may be precisely where the opportunity for change lies for you.

If you feel so upset at that moment that you don't want to talk to the other person, tell them: "I don't want to talk to you right now, please give me a moment to calm down."

Think about whether anything you did or said could have been inappropriate and find the right moment to tell the other person that you are sorry and ask for their forgiveness. Don't say it expecting a response. Your goal for now is just to communicate and gradually verbalize how you feel. You don't have to convince anyone of anything yet.

If you are currently giving the silent treatment, start by giving the other person space and later, or the next day, try to have a conversation that is as casual and fluid as possible, acting relatively normally. When the time is right, after returning to normal daily communication, you can talk about what happened.

You may be one of those people who simply "freeze in silence." This may be because you feel so **trapped in your own discomfort or reactivity** that you find it very difficult to speak, even if you know your partner is suffering. You need to know that the silent treatment becomes a real problem when it becomes a **repetitive pattern with no logical explanation.** If, in addition, you generally do not take responsibility or acknowledge that you have this problem, you need professional help urgently.

We are not anyone's educators; relationships should be between equals. Imposing our thoughts or ideas will not change anyone's behavior. It is not the way to reach an agreement, much less using behavior that is more like blackmail than a search for a solution. We should not think that imposed silence is an educational tool. Sometimes people need to hear what we feel and think to understand each other. We cannot always play at expecting others to read our minds to know what we think and need.

Ignoring someone always damages relationships. Even if we are angry, we must give the people we have a relationship with the opportunity to explain themselves and give their opinion. As we mentioned earlier, silence can be good at first, when emotions are running high, but giving someone the silent treatment hides poor communication skills. Letting problems disappear on their own never works; they are just temporary fixes, and forcing silence doesn't work either.

Using the absence of communication as punishment or to control and modulate someone's behavior is a form of **abuse**, whether done consciously or unconsciously. We are not saying that people do not have the right to end a relationship or contact with someone. We are referring to repeatedly ignoring and denying someone without explanation, with the sole aim of making the other person feel bad and come to us like a submissive animal.

Be empathetic and try to see the situation from the other person's point of view: Once again, we insist on the need to put ourselves in the other person's shoes. How is the other person experiencing our relationship or this conflict? What is going through their mind or heart when they say this or that? How do they feel? Try to empathize with the person and see things from their perspective by examining what happened before the "silent treatment."

Communicate with humility and in the first person. Speaking in the first person is a practical and effective way to share what you think and feel without blaming the other person. This will help you listen actively and assertively. Learn to control and manage your emotions. Control and communication from emotions

Ideally, we should be able **to speak from a place of positive emotions rather than accusations and resentment**. If we focus our dialogue on how we feel and the consequences we may suffer from certain behaviors of another person, we will be opening the door to empathy and listening. If we speak from a place of reproach, we will only provoke defensive attitudes in others and in ourselves when they come back to us.

While it is essential **to respect others in relationships and discussions**, it is also essential to respect ourselves. Therefore, if the silent treatment persists and we are unable to improve communication or other behaviors on the part of the other person, we must set boundaries and not tolerate behaviors that directly harm our emotional well-being.

Monitor your own emotions and avoid saying things motivated by anger.

Ask if you can take a break. If you are too angry or cannot deal with your emotions, tell the person that you want to step away for a moment. This way, you will not ignore them, but you will have time to control yourself. For example, you could say, "I really want to talk about this situation with you. However, my emotions are too intense right now. Can we talk about this in an hour when I feel calmer?"

It's easy to get caught up in our emotions when we feel accused or treated unfairly. You may need to calm down during an argument, but it's a good idea to verbalize how you feel before walking away or refusing to talk to someone.

Focus on the problem. Instead of focusing on the emotions *surrounding* the problem, focus on the problem itself. Don't get sidetracked by things the other person has said that have upset you, but stay on track with what's important. Both of you should work to resolve the problem to figure out how you can move forward. If you're ready to move forward, say, "Can we take a moment to talk about this issue? I'd like to resolve it." If discussions tend to veer off course, you can take a moment, write down your feelings on a piece of paper, and then exchange papers. This way, you can express your emotions without interruption and without getting sidetracked.

Good communication

Tell the person how you feel. Instead of giving them the silent treatment, tell them how their actions made you feel. Stick to "first-person" statements rather than "second-person" statements, as this will help you focus on how you feel rather than placing blame. For example, if you feel upset because your spouse came home late again, you could say, "I feel very anxious when you don't come home on time and don't call. I worry about your safety and miss your company." That's better than saying, "You're never home on time, and I hate it." The first option encourages discussion. The second one assigns blame.

You both need to come to an agreement. Once you have both expressed your complaints, you need to spend some time coming up with ideas for a solution. Of course, that may mean you have to compromise, which means both of you will have to give a little. To reach an agreement, look for the underlying concerns first. Then come up with ways to meet those needs so that both of you benefit.

Listen as much as you talk. To truly communicate, you need to take the time to listen to what the other person is saying and feeling as well. If you reach a point where all you want to do is ignore them, that's probably a sign that you need to have a serious conversation. By listening to what they have to say, you're showing them that you're committed, interested, and respectful. Listen actively to what the person is feeling and thinking, and show them that you are listening by occasionally summarizing what they have said and asking relevant questions.

Don't be afraid to say "I'm sorry." Everyone makes mistakes, but it's important to take responsibility for your actions when you hurt someone. If you handled a situation the wrong way, admit it. Don't be afraid to apologize for any actions you took that caused harm.

Develop better communication skills in therapy. Seeking professional counseling can help if you are interested in becoming a better communicator and if your loved one is also interested. You can do individual, couples, or even family therapy. Participating in therapy can help you identify the roles you both play in the silent treatment and break the cycle of emotional abuse, whether you are dealing with a family member or a spouse.

1. For example, therapy could teach you to find healthier ways to express your demands, such as speaking in the first person, balancing criticism, or asking for a specific time to discuss complaints.
2. On the other hand, you can teach your loved one to express their thoughts and feelings more, as well as how to deal with frustration in better ways than refusing to respond.

Depending on our emotional state, we will have to assess the need to **seek professional help** to guide us on how to better handle arguments and develop assertive communication tools to deal with conflicts. If we feel that our relationship is marked by painful situations like this, we can ask for help, regardless of which side we are on. Psychological therapy can be very useful in teaching you to feel comfortable expressing your opinions, which is the first step to good communication.

Break the silence and communicate, always looking for the simplest solutions. In this case, talk. Don't try to resolve anger or offenses with silence, assuming that the other person can read your mind or should know what's going on because they can't know if you don't express it. It's better to trust yourself, approach the person, and break the silence.

Strengthen your self-esteem. Your problems most likely have an internal root in insecurities and fears that are closely related to your self-esteem and emotion management. Next, we will briefly explore the universe of emotions and communication in emotional relationships. This will allow us to put into practice strategies to improve our emotional management and improve self-knowledge and self-esteem.

C) Guidelines for emotional management and nonviolent communication in emotional relationships

The universe of emotions

We have an innate mechanism that evaluates any stimulus that reaches our senses, and when we assess that something could affect our survival or well-being (or that of those close to us), an emotional response is triggered. This assessment includes the degree to which we evaluate the event as positive or negative, which will produce different emotions. We talk about positive emotions when the event is assessed as progress toward personal goals or well-being. When the event is assessed negatively, it is because there is an obstacle, a danger, a difficulty, an offense, etc., that may endanger our health, well-being, or life.

The same event can be assessed differently depending on the person. An obvious example is a football match. When a goal is scored, the assessment is diametrically different by the fans of the different teams: some are happy and others are sad. Following Rafael Bisquerra in his book *Universo de Emociones (Universe of Emotions)*, we invite you to delve a little deeper into how emotional responses are triggered in human beings so that you can better manage your emotions and communication. When a stimulus is assessed as relevant, it triggers an emotional response. In this case, there is **a triple reaction: neurophysiological, behavioral, and cognitive.**

The **neurophysiological component** consists of responses such as tachycardia, sweating, vasoconstriction, changes in muscle tone, hormonal secretions, changes in the levels of certain neurotransmitters, etc. This neurophysiological or psychophysiological response is what allows us to identify that we are experiencing an emotion.

The **behavioral component** coincides with emotional expression. Observing an individual's behavior allows us to infer what type of emotions they are experiencing. Nonverbal language, mainly facial expressions and tone of voice, provide fairly accurate signals. Voluntary control is possible, but we do not normally pay attention to it and express the emotions we experience spontaneously. Emotional expression can be concealed and can be trained to be concealed. This is important because it allows us to become aware that emotional expression can be learned; it can be regulated at will, with training and practice.

The third component is **cognitive reaction**, which consists of becoming aware of the subjective emotional experience of what is happening inside us. It allows us to become aware of the emotion we are experiencing, which makes it possible to label it, depending on our command of language. For example: "I feel a fear that I cannot control." The limitations of language impose restrictions on our knowledge of what is happening to us in an emotion.

These deficits cause the feeling that "I don't know what's wrong with me." Hence the importance of emotional education aimed at better understanding one's own emotions and their appropriate names, to manage them better. Being able to name emotions is a way of knowing ourselves. Understanding the emotional universe helps us to know the field of possibilities.

The **cognitive component coincides with what is called feeling.** Feeling is emotion made conscious. Once emotion has been made conscious, with the participation of the will, we can lengthen or shorten it in time and intensity. This is emotional regulation. Imagine the difference between prolonging anger, sadness, and anxiety, or shortening those emotions and, in contrast, prolonging joy, love, solidarity, flow, well-being, and happiness.

The important thing about all this is that we can intervene in each of the components of emotion. Intervention in the neurophysiological component involves applying relaxation techniques, breathing, physical control, etc. Education of the behavioral component can include social skills, nuanced expression of emotion, emotional training, smiling, etc. Education of the cognitive component includes introspection, meditation, awareness of emotions, activating the will to regulate emotions, mental training for emotional change, etc.

Developing emotional intelligence

Emotions predispose us to action, but this does not mean that action must necessarily occur. For example, I may feel offended by someone's comment and feel an impulse to respond violently. This predisposition to action can be regulated appropriately. This is very important: the impulsive action I feel like doing does not have to happen. We can regulate our emotions and give an appropriate response, rather than an impulsive one. This is putting intelligence between the stimuli we receive and the response we give. This is emotional intelligence.

An emotion is a complex state of the organism characterized by excitement or disturbance that predisposes us to action. Emotions are generated in response to an external or internal event. The same object can generate different emotions in different people. Emotions are so important in our lives that they become personality traits.

When we think of the people we know, we probably think, "He is a very ...happy, loving, kind, anxious, sad, angry person, etc." In other words, we assign the emotion they most frequently express as a personality trait. A tendency to respond with anger, unrelated to the present situation, is a personality trait.

This means that we build our personality with the emotions we express. And often we are not aware of it. By becoming aware of the importance of emotions in our lives and in our personality, we can ask ourselves: What am I really like? How do others see me? How would I like them to see me? What am I willing to do to be seen as I would like to be?

Self-knowledge, awareness, and emotional regulation

All of this leads us to the importance of self-knowledge, emotional awareness, and emotional regulation. When we apply all of this "emotional astrophysics," we build our personality. When two people meet and one asks, "How are you feeling?" many people simply respond, "Fine." But there are other people who can be more nuanced and may respond: satisfied, excited, cheerful, in love, happy, indignant, anxious, sad, disappointed, frustrated, etc. The list can be extended to more than five hundred possible words that describe emotions that can be used to explain how we feel.

It is important to clarify that **all emotions are good**. The problem lies in what we do with our emotions. How we manage them determines the effects they will have on our well-being and that of others. But while all emotions are good, some make us feel good and others make us feel bad. This is why some are called positive and others negative, depending on whether or not they contribute to our well-being.

Emotional management practices

Below, we suggest some tools and guidelines to improve your emotional management, starting with identifying and recognizing your emotions. This is very useful whether you are a victim of the silent treatment or someone who uses it. Remember that in emotional relationships, what matters most is our emotional well-being, and we always have a part to play in achieving it.

"Our inner dialogue"

In this exercise, we talk about the conversation we constantly have with ourselves, which is not always based on reality. In most cases, they are based on our interpretations of reality. Distorting reality can cause unwanted emotional states, leading to sadness, submission, and even aggression. One possible solution would be to look at what you want to see. Focus your energy on thoughts that help you improve your relationship and prevent unnecessary suffering for yourself and the other person.

Practical application: Become aware of your inner dialogue. We call these constant, repetitive thoughts that constantly affect us "rumination." You can do avoid this through *mindfulness* practices.

1. Analyze whether what you are saying to yourself is hurting you or what emotion it is provoking.
2. Check if it is useful.
3. Create a new inner dialogue aimed at making you feel better.

Example:

1. I realize that I have a constant thought in which I say to myself, "My partner doesn't pay enough attention to me despite how much I love her. I've sacrificed a lot to be with her and give her everything she needs, and yet instead of staying with me, she goes out for coffee with her friends every Friday.
2. It makes me feel bad, sad, as if I've been abandoned and despised.
3. This thought is not helping me at all. If she has gone out, maybe she needs to or enjoys being with other people or doing other things without me, and maybe I should also take the opportunity to do things for myself.
4. I tell myself, "She also has the right to have time to be with her friends, even if it's hard for me to admit. It doesn't do me any good to feel abandoned, and it's not true because she'll come back to be with me much more than with her friends. There's no point in feeling bad about it."

Identifying our emotions

Practice identifying your emotions below. Naming what we feel helps us manage our emotions.

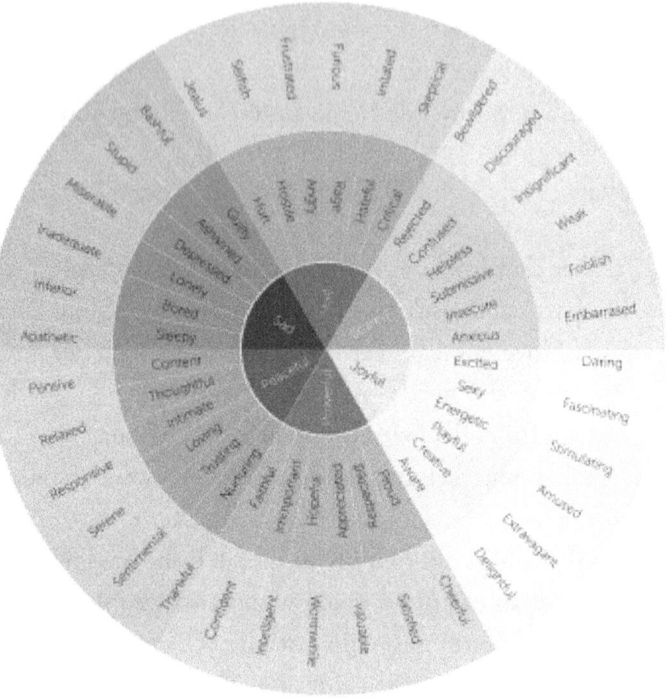

Nonviolent communication

Human beings are very speculative, and so it is easy **to jump to conclusions that damage relationships**. When we have a problem with someone, it is usually because of a misunderstanding. Each person is unique, and we live immersed in a myriad of problems and situations that we do not always share with those around us.

Talking is the only way to **avoid misunderstandings** and resolve differences. It is better to discuss and talk than to remain silent. By remaining silent, we are avoiding confrontation and putting ourselves on the defensive, which makes us feel threatened and, as a result, our happiness suffers.

Talking about issues that have hurt us is not pleasant, but it is a better and more effective solution than remaining silent and letting our minds spin and invent responses that are not real. A psychologist will always recommend talking and, above all, **clarifying feelings** and never hiding behind silence.

Nonviolent Communication (NVC) is a tool for communicating more effectively using empathy and resolving conflicts without violence or coercion. NVC was developed by Marshall Rosenberg, a psychologist and mediator who studied the relationship between violence and the use of judgmental and evaluative language. He asserts that the ultimate cause of violence lies in the way we think, communicate, and manage power relationships. (ACNV; Association for Nonviolent Communication). It involves changing our mindset based on judgments and static norms, on what is right and wrong, to a method based on honest expression and empathetic listening, seeking the satisfaction of all parties. Which would you prefer, to be right or to be happy? You can't have both at the same time. NVC seeks the best way to satisfy our needs and live in harmony with others. To this end, it proposes a four-step process:

1. We observe the specific actions that are affecting our well-being.
2. We identify our feelings in relation to what we observe.
3. We identify the unmet needs that are causing those feelings.
4. We clearly ask the other person what we would like them to do.

Jackals and giraffes

Rosenberg chose these two animals (both for their appearance and for certain aspects of their behavior) to illustrate two different ways of communicating. The jackal represents a way of thinking and expressing oneself based on moral judgments, while the giraffe represents empathy and awareness of one's own needs and those of others. Jackal language is full of labels. When someone does something they don't like, they label them as "mean" or "stupid." They also judge their own behavior harshly. Expressions such as "I'm stupid" or "I should have done..." are common, so their self-esteem is very low.

Jackals do not try to understand the feelings or needs of others and try to change their behavior using punishment and rewards. Unfortunately, when we get someone to do what we want out of fear, guilt, or shame, they are likely to harbor resentment that can work against us in the future. Another aspect of jackal language is that it denies responsibility for our decisions, with phrases such as "I have to..." or "I'm forced by the rules," which hide the possibility of choice.

In giraffe language, there is no "right" or "wrong." Reality is changing, so instead of resorting to these static classifications, giraffes try to connect with their emotions and ask others for what they need to enrich their lives, without judgment or demands. They also take into account the needs of others.

Giraffes are aware that we always have a choice. When circumstances leave them with two unappealing options, they make a decision with empathy, connecting with the needs they hope to satisfy. If they regret an action, they remember the needs they were trying to meet when they took it, and try to learn from it to find better strategies.

Most of us have been raised like jackals. Our judgmental, obligation-based way of thinking is a result of the hierarchical society we live in. NVC can help us change our mindset, think, speak, and act like giraffes.

Observe without evaluating

When we observe without evaluating, we remain faithful to the facts, to what we see and hear. We do not judge, label, compare, assume, or distort what has happened in any way. We take special care not to confuse observation with evaluation, because if we mix them up, the other person will surely hear criticism. A pure observation is "Antonio spoke three times without waiting for his turn at this afternoon's meeting." Saying, for example, "Antonio doesn't let us speak" is interpreting the facts. If we say, "John always interrupts," we are generalizing.

Identify our feelings

We focus on what is alive in us at this moment. What emotions do we feel in relation to the events we observe? Sometimes this is not easy, as we have a much richer vocabulary for labeling others than for describing our feelings. Listing feelings can help. Some expressions such as "deceived" or "rejected" are false feelings, because instead of describing our emotions, they hide an evaluation of what other people have done. We often hide our feelings for fear of what others will think of us, but expressing them helps us establish an empathetic connection.

Becoming aware of our needs

It is not other people who cause our emotions, but rather they depend on our interpretation of events, our thoughts, and our expectations. Needs are revealed through feelings. If they are satisfied, they are pleasant; if they are not pleasant, it is because they are warning us that we need to address an unmet need. Listing human needs can help us identify them. It is important not to confuse needs with strategies, because we can make the mistake of thinking that they can only be met in a certain way or by a single person. There are many strategies for satisfying a need.

What we ask of others

Once we have analyzed and expressed how we feel, we make a specific, achievable, and negotiable request. We clearly state what we would like them to do, rather than focusing on what we do not want them to do. Giving someone the opportunity to satisfy a need is like giving them a gift, because human beings like to contribute to the well-being of others. We can also direct the request to ourselves. It is important to make it clear to the other person that we only want them to agree to what we are asking if they want to. If we are not prepared to accept a negative response, we are making a demand. When we perceive that something is being demanded of us, our empathy is blocked.

Empathetic listening

When we receive a message, we try to identify the other person's observations, feelings, needs, and requests (the 4 steps), even if they speak to us with judgments and demands. We can try to guess how they feel and ask to verify it, or paraphrase what they say to encourage them to continue expressing themselves. Before we divert our attention to finding a solution to the conflict, it is a good idea to take the time to listen.

Showing someone that we understand them improves their willingness to seek a joint strategy. Offering empathy to someone means giving them our full attention. It means not judging them or forming an opinion about what they say. It simply means being present. Some things we do regularly, such as giving advice, downplaying, or explaining what we think about what they are telling us, make it difficult to connect empathetically. When you are in the middle of an intense discussion, it can be helpful to shift your attention to listening fully to the other person. They will see that you are paying attention, that you are listening, and they may begin to calm down.

Ask for time to discuss the issue. People who give someone the silent treatment are basically sending signals about what they need because they can't communicate their needs effectively. Your friend or partner may not be trying to hurt you by pulling away. Instead, they may be trying to heal their own wounds after an argument.

Take the easy route and do what they can't: choose a time to discuss the issue like adults. Say, "We're both acting emotionally right now and need some time to think. How about we give it a few hours and come back at 3 p.m. to finish this discussion?" Acting this way prevents the ice from having an impact because you agree to have a silence. Then, when you've both gained some objectivity, try to resolve the misunderstanding.

Try to see the situation from the other person's point of view. Keep in mind that communication is a two-way street. If your loved one feels the need to avoid you or shut down communication, they must be hurting. Try to empathize with that person and see things from their perspective. Examine the exchange that preceded the silent treatment and consider what you said. What did you respond with? If you were in their shoes, how would you feel? If you are still bothered by the fact that the person is not talking to you, try talking to a trusted friend or relative to get an outside perspective on the situation. Be sure to choose someone who will be honest and kind to you.

Speak in the first person during an argument. The silent treatment is a passive-aggressive method that can also trigger passive aggression in you. The other person refuses to share their feelings or have a conversation, so you decide to ignore them too. Instead, use an assertive method that can help you get your message across without making the situation worse.

Speaking in the first person is a practical way to share what you think and feel without blaming the other person. You could say, "When you ignore me, I feel small and powerless. I would like us to share our feelings more actively and not walk away. Next time, could you ask for some space instead of just ignoring me?" While talking to that person, be sure to lead by example and respond with kindness, humility, respect, and self-control. Avoid accusing them or assuming what their intentions might be.

Learning to manage our emotions and relationships for mutual happiness is within our reach. It just depends on putting the right tools in place to enjoy the people around us in complete freedom and without emotional attachment or dependence. All human beings seek happiness.

The silent treatment is the opposite of loving speech and deep listening, two extraordinary methods for opening the door to communication with our loved ones. We should not use the language of authority and reproach, but rather the language of love and understanding.

Practice active listening as much as possible. Sometimes people will say things that surprise you. They may say something that goes against your way of seeing things. When we listen with our hearts, we begin to see and understand the other person more deeply and understand them better.

Conclusion

A thorough analysis of the **silent treatment** reveals that it is not a simple lack of communication or a bad character trait, but a serious and deliberate form of emotional abuse with profound psychological, neurological, and relational consequences. By activating the brain's pain centers and exploiting evolutionary fears of abandonment, silence becomes a weapon capable of eroding self-esteem, destroying trust, and leaving lasting scars on its victims.

The distinction between a healthy "time out," intended for self-regulation, and the silent treatment, whose purpose is punishment and control, is fundamental. Understanding this difference is the first step for victims to validate their experience and stop blaming themselves for the abuser's behavior.

For those who are the targets of this abuse, the road to recovery involves a combination of strategies: staying calm so as not to feed the manipulation, using assertive communication to set firm boundaries, and, most importantly, focusing on self-care and depersonalizing the attack. Seeking professional help is crucial when the behavior is a pattern rooted in a dynamic of abuse.

For those who employ the silent treatment, change is possible, but it requires a courageous exercise in self-awareness, taking responsibility for the harm caused, and an active commitment to learning healthier ways of managing emotions and communicating needs. Therapy is often an indispensable component of this process.

Finally, mindfulness and self-compassion practices emerge as essential therapeutic tools for victims. These are not passive solutions, but acts of active resistance that allow the person to regulate their nervous system, rebuild their sense of worth, and reclaim agency over their own internal state. Healing from the silent treatment is a process of relearning how to inhabit a safe inner space, replacing the echo of silence with the voice of self-compassion, and reaffirming the fundamental right of every human being to be seen, heard, and treated with dignity.

One last wish

If you have found this book useful, please help me to increase the number of people who live and love healthily.

Thank you for taking a minute of your time to **review the book.** It is a valuable contribution that will help and guide future readers.

Thank you very much for your collaboration.

Cheers, good luck, and love

Bibliography

Association for Nonviolent Communication. ACNV [1]

Halpern, Daniel, Sebastián Venezuela, and James E. Katz. "Selfie-ists" or "Narci-selfiers"?: A cross-lagged panel analysis of selfie taking and narcissism. [2]*Personality and Individual Differences.*[3] Volume 97, July 2016, Pages 98-101

Johnson, Stephen M. (1987). *Humanizing the Narcissistic Style*. Publisher: W.W.Norton.

Ni, Preston. How to Successfully Handle Narcissists[4]. PNCC. (2014)

Ni, Preston. A Practical Guide for Narcissists to Change Towards the Higher Self.[5] PNCC. (2015)

Ni, Preston. Understanding Narcissism's Destructive Impact on Relationships — An Indispensable Reader[6]. PNCC. (2018)

MacDonald, Pat (2014) *Narcissism in the modern world*, Psychodynamic Practice, 20:2, 144-153, DOI: 10.1080/14753634.2014.894225[7]

---

1. https://www.asociacioncomunicacionnoviolenta.org/
2. https://www.sciencedirect.com/science/journal/01918869
3. *https://www.sciencedirect.com/science/journal/01918869*
4. http://nipreston.com/new/publications/
5. http://nipreston.com/new/publications/
6. http://nipreston.com/new/publications/
7. https://doi.org/10.1080/14753634.2014.894225

Punset, Eduardo, Rafael Bisquerra. (2015) *Universo de emociones.* Editorial Palaugea.

Riso, Walter. (2012). *Enamórate de ti: El valor imprescindible de la autoestima*. Editorial Zenit.

About the author

Sophia Bengal Ph. D., is an experienced advisor, also master's degree holder in communication, as well as a tireless researcher. She is the founder and director of ***Revolucionamorarte*** (revolucionamorarte.com[1]), a space to learn how to love yourself and others as a source of real and genuine happiness.

We can all be happy, give and receive "true love."

1. https://revolucionamorarte.com/

www.ingramcontent.com/pod-product-compliance
Lightning Source LLC
LaVergne TN
LVHW050827061126
851857LV00012B/1013

* 9 7 9 8 2 3 5 7 4 1 2 4 9 *

Endnotes

Chapter 1

[1]Nick Saban, Nick Saban Leadership Clinic, University of Alabama

Chapter 2

[2]Kirby Smart, Post game press conference, Georgia vs. Florida, October 2021

Chapter 3

[3]Bill Belichick, Do Your Job - NFL Films / Patriots Documentary

Chapter 4

[4] Tom Brady, Tom Brady: The TB12 Method 2017

Chapter 5

[5]Nick Saban, Nick Saban Coaching Clinic and repeated in his book How Good Do You Want to Be?

Chapter 6

[6]Tom Brady, Tom Brady Interview, Super Bowl Media Week (2015), also quoted in The TB12 Method.

Chapter 7

[7]Patrick Mahomes, AFC Championship Post Game Interview (2023), referencing Billie Jean King's famous line.

Chapter 8

[8]Paul "Bear" Bryant, Bear Bryant Coaching Philosophy, widely cited from his speeches at Alabama coaching clinics and documented in Bear Bryant on Leadership.

Chapter 9

[9]Tom Brady, Source: Tom Brady Interview, ESPN E:60 Feature (2013).

Chapter 10

[10]Mike Alstott, Source: Mike Alstott Football Life — NFL Films document

Bonus Story

[11]Fleetwod Mac, *Go Your Own Way,* https://www.azlyrics.com/lyrics/fleetwood mac/goyourownway.html, retrieved 8/3/26.

www.ingramcontent.com/pod-product-compliance
Lightning Source LLC
LaVergne TN
LVHW050825061126
851857LV00012B/985
9781953241931